Listening Hearts

RETREAT DESIGNS
AND MEDITATION EXERCISES

With Guidelines for Retreat Leaders
and Covenant Groups

by Suzanne G. Farnham
Photographs by Paul Hotvedt

MOREHOUSE PUBLISHING

To Barney, the most important person in my life.

Cover design based on an illustration by Megan Murphy

Copyright © 1994 by the Christian Vocation Project, Inc.

Second Printing, 1996

Morehouse Publishing
P.O. Box 1321
Harrisburg, PA 17105

The Eucharistic Prayers, "Incarnation," "Invitation," and "Pilgrims," are reprinted by kind permission of John Mossi, S.J., who is the copyright holder. They have been adapted by Suzanne Farnham from *Bread Blessed and Broken* (Paulist Press, 1974).

Library of Congress Cataloging-in-Publication Data
Farnham, Suzanne G.
    Listening hearts: retreat designs, with meditation exercises and leader guidelines / by Suzanne Farnham: photographs by Paul Hotvedt.
        p.   cm.
    ISBN 0-8192-1621-6 (pbk.)
    1. Retreats   I. Title.
BX2375.F37   1994
269'.6—dc20
                                                94-8963
                                                CIP

Printed in the United States of America

CONTENTS

ACKNOWLEDGMENTS

Everything I write as part of the Christian Vocation Project is the fruit of a vast network of people who bountifully contribute time, talent, hard work, professional expertise, and money to this shared endeavor that seeks to make widespread the practice of discernment in the Church. This book would not be possible without the gracious help of many.

A few people in particular have been crucial to the preparation of this book:

Adele B. Free and Louise E. Miller, who manage the day-to-day operations of the organization, which has freed me to prepare this material for publication.

Marilynn E. Cornejo, who has spent hours on the computer — far beyond the call of duty — to make my not-so-neat handwritten work presentable for the publisher.

John E. McIntyre, who brings both a mastery of the English language and knowledge of Scripture and spiritual theology to his ministry of editing our copy.

Paul B. Hotvedt, who did the photography for this book.

Chris L. Hotvedt, who served as book designer.

And John Mossi, S. J., who graciously gave permission to adapt and publish three Great Thanksgivings from his book *Bread Blessed and Broken* to use with these retreat designs.

Most especially I thank God, who touches the hearts of so many to give generously of themselves to this work.

INTRODUCTION

Retreats provide a time, place, and structure to draw a group of people into God's presence. Retreats offer a setting in which participants can let ideas about God flow from their minds into their hearts to be assimilated into their lives individually and collectively. The retreats in this book, based on the book *Listening Hearts*, also teach a variety of approaches to meditation that can be used by retreatants in their continuing spiritual quests.

The retreat designs and Guidelines for Leaders for the "Retreat on Call, Ministry, and Discernment" and the "Retreat on Community" in this book are intended as a resource for experienced retreat leaders. But the meditation exercises within these two retreats can be used by individuals as part of their private devotional lives. In yet another vein, the "Group Rock Garden" is a self-conducted retreat that makes it possible for a small group of people to organize and lead a retreat for themselves.

Hence, the retreats and meditation exercises herein serve to help both individuals and communities integrate the practice of discernment into their daily lives.

Amen.

USING THE MEDITATION EXERCISES FOR PRIVATE PRAYER

The exercises in the "Retreat on Call, Ministry, and Discernment" can be used privately by individuals. The considerable benefits of sharing the experience in a community of faith could be lost, but need not be. The leaven of a community can be acquired by recruiting one, two, or three other people to use the same exercises for their own spiritual discipline and then agree to meet together periodically to share reflections and serve as a support group for one another. Doing these exercises one at a time over an extended period of time permits making use of all of the options provided — which can expand the experience considerably.

An hour is a good amount of time to set aside for each meditation period. Put the time on your calendar and treat it as a commitment. Assemble the needed supplies beforehand.

Develop a simple format that includes:
   (1) A period of preparation.
   (2) The meditation exercise.
   (3) A closing portion.

The preparation period can include singing or reading the hymn suggested for opening the retreat session — or else a centering prayer such as, "Holy Spirit, live in me," repeated many times over. Time for reviewing the appointed chapter of *Listening Hearts* also makes a suitable component for this preparatory segment. The closing portion can include time for reflecting on the meditation exercise, offering prayers, and possibly reading or singing the closing hymn listed for the retreat session.

You can approach the "*Listening Hearts* Retreat on Community" in a like manner. If working on a sand tray or mobile, use three, four, or five sessions for the one meditation exercise. Another possibility with this retreat material is to set aside a day, or at least the major portion of a day, to consolidate a given option into one extended meditation session. This can be a particularly good way to go about the Contemplative Sand Tray exercise, making a day trip to a wooded stream or river, and taking a picnic lunch along with you.

When gathering with a support group to share reflections, try to establish a quiet, reflective atmosphere. Make sure that each member of the group gets an equal opportunity to participate. The Thomas Merton Prayer at the end of *Listening Hearts* makes a suitable prayer for opening and/or closing the meeting. You may want to agree to keep what is said confidential so that people are likely to speak more freely. A support group to provide a communal dimension is almost essential when doing the meditation exercises from the "Retreat on Community."

LEADING *LISTENING HEARTS* RETREATS FOR GROUPS

Both the "*Listening Hearts* Retreat on Call, Ministry, and Discernment" and the "*Listening Hearts* Retreat on Community" call for an experienced group leader who is accustomed to silence and meditation. The suggestions spelled out below apply to both of these retreats. Specific guidelines for conducting each of the two retreats appear at the rear of this book. Prospective leaders may want to look over the leaders' guidelines for each retreat prior to reading the design for that retreat.

PREPARATION OF LEADERS

1.   As a general form of preparation, become familiar with the book *Listening Hearts*, including the endnotes and appendices, and with all of the retreat material.

2.   Prayer is an important part of preparation. Intensify your prayer as the time draws near. Your prayerfulness will set the tone for the program. Pray for the program and for the individual participants.

3.   Using the Supplies Checklist for the retreat you are leading, procure all the supplies you need well ahead of time.

4.   If using music cassettes, practice the music <u>with</u> the cassettes. You need to be familiar with the recordings and able to sing with them. If you can line up a live musician who is capable of playing some or all of the music well, by all means do so. Ideally, meet with any musicians ahead of time to run through the music. It can be a good safety net to have the tapes and cassette player with you as a back-up. Make sure the cassettes are wound to the proper side beforehand.

5.   If you are working with a partner, spend time planning how you will work together: You need to have your signals straight; you also need time together to get "in sync" with each other.

6.   Select a space that is free of such interruptions as phones, doorbells, and people walking through the room during the retreat.

7.   Try to prepare an attractive, informal, meditative environment. Arrange chairs in a circle to help establish a sense of community. Arrive well ahead of time to set up so that everything is ready before others arrive.

8.   As the director of the retreat, make every effort to begin and end on schedule. It is important to end at the appointed time unless the entire group agrees to a revised closing time. Within the overall framework, estimate the time for each session and for each segment within the session, but do not adhere rigidly to this internal time schedule.

9.   Make your plan, but be fluid. Let the Holy Spirit lead you. Listen with the ear of your heart. You can add, subtract, switch or abbreviate hymns to accommodate the situation. You can allow more time in one place and consolidate things elsewhere if the reasons are compelling. But also be ready to intervene and move things on when that is what is needed. Keep aware of the stated objectives and do not depart from them without careful consideration.

PREPARATION OF PARTICIPANTS

The relationship between the preparation of the group and the success of the program is strong. Participants need to read *Listening Hearts* beforehand, especially the parts on which their retreat is based. They need their own copies of the book sufficiently ahead of time to read the material and mark the portions (a) that speak strongly to them, (b) that they do not understand, and (c) with which they disagree. They need to bring their books with them. It is the responsibility of the leaders to communicate this information to the participants in an emphatic way.

REFRESHMENTS

If you plan to begin with a dinner, make sure that the arrangements are taken care of and that the plans are clear to the participants.

As an alternative, you may want to schedule a short refreshment period just before the retreat begins — twenty minutes or half an hour for people to unwind, to say hello to those they know, and to meet anyone they may not know. Most especially, it gives the leaders an opportunity to meet everyone.

Cheese, fruit, and tea make a good menu. Rich, sweet desserts can make people sleepy.

Unless the group is very small, it may help to have everyone wear name tags.

HYMNS

Hymns are sung prayers. As Saint Augustine said, the person who sings prays twice. If the leader conveys these ideas to the group, it may encourage them to pay closer attention to the words of the hymns.

The hymns were selected to reinforce the themes of the retreats. They come from a variety of traditions. Stylistic diversity has benefits, but if some of the hymns do not seem suited to a particular group, the leader may select other hymns, attempting to find ones that are equally appropriate to the substance of the retreat.

All the hymns for these retreats may be found in the *Listening Hearts SONGBOOK*. People can benefit from standing for hymns as a kind of "seventh-inning stretch." Chants, however, are meant to slow us down and make us reflective; they are best performed sitting.

CLOSING EUCHARISTS

Designs are provided for closing Eucharists for those who want to conclude their retreats with the Eucharist. If a Eucharist is on Sunday, use the texts indicated in the lectionary rather than the Scripture suggested in this book. Whatever Scripture is read, invite the group to reflect on those texts in relation to their retreat experience. Arrange for an authorized minister to preside at the liturgy.

Prior to the retreat, make copies of the Order of Service sheet (entitled CLOSING EUCHARIST) for the Eucharist. Highlight a sheet to mark the appropriate portions for each person to whom you will be assigning a specific part. You may assign the following responsibilities:

- Announcing the hymns
- Reading the Thomas Merton Prayer
- Reading the 1st reading
- Reading the 2nd reading
- Opening and closing the reflection period
- Introducing and concluding the prayers
- Presenting the bread
- Presenting the wine and water
- Offering thanks for Communion
- Giving the dismissal

During the Announcements of the session that precedes the Eucharist, explain the plan for the Eucharist and feedback forms. Distribute the service sheets and make sure that each participant understands his or her instructions. Indicate that there will be a short silent break after the next hymn to give participants time to go off and prepare for the Eucharist. Ask the group to return to the circle as soon as they are ready. Have the Eucharist in the circle, using a small table as the altar, unless you prefer another location.

Retreat on Call, Ministry, and Discernment

OBJECTIVES

To spend time present to God.
To reflect on call, ministry, and discernment as they relate to our own lives.
To deepen the bonds of Christian community.

Listening Hearts Retreat on Call, Ministry, and Discernment

CONTENTS

Orientation Session

Meditation Session   "The Introduction"

Meditation Session   "Call and Ministry"

Meditation Session   "Discernment"

Meditation Session   "Helpful Conditions"

Meditation Session   "Is It God Speaking?"

Closing Eucharist

Great Thanksgiving: Invitation
                                  Pilgrims

Feedback Form

Supplies Checklist

Introductory Segment For Optional Second Retreat

ORIENTATION SESSION

Hymn
"Spirit, Be Our Spirit"

Greetings

Introductions

1. Please introduce yourself by name.

2. Then respond to a few of these questions:

   What do you consider your primary work?

   Do you ever hear God in silence?

   Do you hear God through people?

   Does God seem to speak to you through the events of your life?

   Do you hear God speaking through art? dance? drama? nature? literature? music? your senses? your imagination? your dreams? your pain? pleasure?

   Does God reach you through Scripture? liturgy? Communion?

   Are there other ways God communicates with you?

   If you do not want to respond to these questions say, "I pass."

3. Nod to the person to your left when you are through.

Overview

SESSION: "THE INTRODUCTION"

Hymn
"Be Still and Know"

Exercise

*Find a place in your heart and speak there with
the Lord. It is the Lord's reception room.*
Words of Theophan the Recluse
Ware, *The Art of Prayer*
(*Listening Hearts*, p.1)

In silence, slowly read and reread the above words until they take root at the center of your being.

Then feel the words within yourself as you focus on the flame that has been placed at the center of the circle.

Period Of Silence

Chant
"Stay Here and Keep Watch"

Shared Reflections

Thomas Merton Prayer

Announcements

Hymn
"Jacob's Ladder Sequel"

SESSION: "CALL AND MINISTRY"

BASED ON CHAPTERS 1 & 2

Hymn
"Jesus Calls Us"

Gathering Time

Exercise

Option A

Morning by morning he wakens…
wakens my ear to listen as those who are taught.
The Lord has opened my ear….

Isaiah 50:4-5

1. Select a quiet, comfortable space.
2. Take the circumstances of your daily life into your meditation with you, especially any question or issue with which you may be wrestling.
3. Silently say the above passage over and over to yourself, taking the words into your body, mind, and soul.
4. Eventually you may (but not necessarily) consolidate the passage into a few words or even one word.
5. Finally, let yourself fall still.

- Take coloring pens. Express your feelings in colors. Express your feelings through the movement of the pens. It does not matter what it looks like; the objective is to communicate with God and yourself. You are not required to show others. When done, silently gaze at your drawing if time permits.

and/or

- Take pen and paper. Write a stream-of-consciousness passage, expressing your feelings in words without thinking about what is coming out and without concern about grammar, sentence structure, spelling or punctuation. When finished, become still again.

Option B

Whoever serves me must follow me, and where I am, there will my servant be also….

John 12:26

Use the above passage as a springboard for your thoughts, a place to begin, a reference point. Or select any small segment of Chapter 2 as your text.

- Draw a religious symbol such as a cross, a circle, a butterfly, a river. Then sit in silence with your symbol as a focal point. Meditate on the text you chose.

and/or

- Select a hymn tune or some simple melody. Write a short hymn or song based on your thoughts and feelings about ministry, especially in relation to your own life.

Session: "Call and Ministry"
(continued)

Shared Reflections

Informal Prayers

Thomas Merton Prayer

Announcements

Hymn
"Lord, You Give the Great Commission"

SESSION: "DISCERNMENT"

BASED ON CHAPTER 3

Chant
"Changeless and Changing"

Gathering Time

Exercise

I will instruct you and teach you the way you should go; I will counsel you with my eye upon you.

Ps. 32:8

...the word is very near you; it is in your mouth and in your heart, so that you can do it.

Deut. 30:14

Option A

1. Take a bag of clay, a paper plate, and a chopstick.

2. Find a comfortable place to work with the clay. Put the clay on the plate to keep it clean.

3. Take time to offer yourself and the issues of your life to God in prayer.

4. Select one of the above passages. Read it over and over until the words permeate you.

5. Begin to express your feelings in the clay. Dig, pound, hold it, rub it gently. Etch it, roll it, or break it in pieces. Let the clay and your actions speak to you. Let God speak to you through the clay and your actions. For instance, the clay may be hard and cold when you begin. The warmth of your hands may make it more supple. This may suggest something to you.

Alternate between working with the clay and quietly looking at it in contemplation.

Try to experience this as prayer, as communication with God. Whether or not you create a recognizable object does not matter.

Option B

1. Take pen and paper.

2. Find a quiet comfortable place.

3. Offer yourself and the issues of your life to God.

4. Select one of the above Scripture passages.

5. Silently meditate on the passage.

6. Then begin to write a poem; it does not have to be in rhyme or meter. Or you may write a stream-of-consciousness passage; this entails writing down whatever comes to you without censoring it — not thinking about punctuation, spelling, neatness, or what it means.

7. Read over what you have written and just absorb it for a while.

Session: "Discernment"
(continued)

Shared Reflections

Informal Prayers

Thomas Merton Prayer

Announcements

Chant
"Changeless and Changing"

SESSION: "HELPFUL CONDITIONS"
BASED ON CHAPTER 4

Hymn
"Guide Us Another Day"

Gathering Time

Exercise

Option A	Option B
1. Take some time to look over Chapter 4 and select one of the Scripture passages quoted there. Use the selected passage or a few words extracted from it as your meditation text.	1. Join up with one or two other people.
	2. Together select one of the sections set apart within Chapter 4. Allow time for everyone to carefully review the designated section.
2. Take a brisk walk by yourself and/or find a place to sit quietly. In your heart, repeat the selected words over and over. Perhaps incorporate them into your breathing.	3. Take a walk together, talking about the thoughts expressed in that particular section, especially as they relate to your own lives. Or else find a secluded place to sit together and reflect aloud on the selected passage.

Shared Reflections

Informal Prayers

Thomas Merton Prayer

Announcements

Hymn
"How Firm a Foundation"

SESSION: "IS IT GOD SPEAKING?"

BASED ON CHAPTER 5

Chant

"God's Mysterious Threads Combining"

Gathering Time

Exercise

Find a quiet comfortable spot. Use the entire chapter as your text, but especially consider the signs of call enumerated on pages 46 through 48. Take your reflections from the exercises on the previous chapters and any issues with which you wrestle into your meditation with you.

Option A	Option B	Option C
Meditate by writing • a dialogue with God • a dialogue among characters • or a prayer	Take several pieces of connected computer paper. Meditate on the chapter and your life by drawing a series of pictures (which can be abstract).	Collect objects indoors and out; cut out pictures from newspapers and magazines. Construct a collage on construction paper, a piece of board or some other flat surface. Magazines, newspapers, construction paper, scissors and glue are on the supply table.

Shared Reflections

Informal Prayers

Thomas Merton Prayer

Announcements

Hymn

"Surprise Is Always Part of God's Call"

Feedback Forms

Hymn

"Jacob's Ladder Sequel"

CLOSING EUCHARIST

HYMN   *"Spirit of the Living God"*

THOMAS MERTON PRAYER

Stand to read. Begin with "Let us pray."
Read the Thomas Merton Prayer on the last
page of *Listening Hearts.*

READINGS:
  1. Ecclesiasticus 2:1-11
  2. Luke 6:20-36

Readers stand to read. Announce the
reading and invite people to follow it in their
Bibles. Give people time to find the passage.
Conclude with "This is the word of the Lord."

REFLECTION PERIOD

Appointed person invites the group to reflect
on the Scripture passages in relation to their
meditations in the course of the retreat and
to offer their thoughts and feelings aloud if so
moved. Allows time for people to reflect and
to speak should they want to. Then concludes
by standing and offering a prayer that ties
together the Scripture and the reflection
time, punctuated with a loud "AMEN" at
the end.

HYMN   *"Brooding Breath of God"*

PRAYERS

Appointed person invites the congregation
to offer their prayers, silently or aloud.
Permits time for free and open participation.
Then draws the prayers together in some
way, concluding with a hearty "AMEN."

PEACE

Presiding priest initiates by proclaiming:
"The peace of the Lord be always with you."

OFFERTORY:
  Bread & Wine

One person presents bread as another
presents the water and wine.

  Doxology

GREAT THANKSGIVING	"Invitation" or "Pilgrims"
LORD'S PRAYER	
COMMUNION	
THANKSGIVING FOR COMMUNION	Appointed person offers a short prayer of thanks for Communion.
HYMN *"Seek Ye First"*	Can be sung in canon.
DISMISSAL	As a charge to the congregation, in a hearty voice the appointed person offers two or three sentences that capture the thrust of the weekend and challenge participants to take the message of the retreat into their daily lives. Concludes with "Go in peace, rejoicing in the power of the Spirit."

GREAT THANKSGIVING: INVITATION

Glorious God, we thank you for continually extending your call to us
    even when we fail to answer.
We thank you for approaching us in different ways
    tailored to our personalities.

We thank you for calling Jacob,
    who first wrestled with your messenger
    and yielded to the power of your love;
for Jeremiah, who tried to ignore your presence
    but found your persistent calling impossible to refuse;
for Isaiah, who accepted your difficult invitation
    to return Israel to your praise;
for Elijah who heard your sound in the movement
    of cool winds and gentle breezes;
for John the Baptist, who was led by your Spirit
    to fearlessly preach the coming of the Lord;
for your Son's calling of ordinary people like
    Andrew and Peter,
    Martha and Mary,
    AND US.
We thank you,
    for you still invite people to share in your life.

And so, with hearts full of love,
    we join with your saints in proclaiming your praise:
        Holy, holy, holy Lord,
        God of power and might,
        Heaven and earth are full of your glory.
        Hosanna in the highest.
        Blessed is the one who comes in the name of the Lord.
        Hosanna in the highest.

We bless you for the life of Jesus
    who gradually came to realize
    the dimensions of your call.
In the temple,
    he spoke your word to the elders of the land.

In the desert,
　　he was tempted to power, honor, and glory,
　　but chose obedience to your will.
In towns and villages,
　　he forgave sinners
　　and preached your kingdom of mercy and justice.
When lawyers and scribes tried to test him,
　　your Son responded with a new commandment of love.

On the night before he died, Jesus
　　asked that the cup of Gethsemane be withdrawn.
But in response to your bidding he drank that cup
　　just as earlier in the evening
　　he gave us the cup of life everlasting.

Gathered with his friends at table, Jesus took bread and blessed you.
He broke the bread and shared it, saying:
Take and eat.
This is my body which will be given up for you.

Then he took the cup, blessed you again, and said:
Take and drink. This is the cup of the new covenant in my blood
　　which is poured out for you and for all people.
Do this in memory of me.

Father, we joyfully remember
　　that the cup of the table
　　overcame the cup of the garden,
　　for your Son not only died but rose
　　that we might have life.
To help us respond to your call
　　and guide us in your ways
　　he has sent the Holy Spirit as your gift.

Let us proclaim our life in your Spirit:
　　When we eat this bread and drink this cup,
　　we proclaim your death, Lord Jesus,
　　until you come in glory.

We ask that your Spirit
    may continue to fill us with your grace.
May our ears, eyes, and hearts
    be open to your summons, to your call.

Be mindful of your people;
    especially be present to those who are imprisoned,
    tormented by illness, physical and mental,
    and who find it difficult to hear and to respond.
Help us to find you
    in stillness and in turmoil,
    in pleasure and in business.
May we always imitate the care and concern
    of your son who is the Savior of the world.

Through whom,
with whom,
in whom,
in the unity of the Holy Spirit,
all glory and honor is yours,
All Loving God,
forever and ever.
Amen.

George Sullivan, S.J. and John Mossi, S.J., adapted

GREAT THANKSGIVING: PILGRIMS

Gracious God, beloved companion of pilgrims,
    we gather to praise and bless you.
Your name is faithful one and your love is
    everlasting.
We have come to experience your love in many ways
    as life's pilgrims.

We thank you for the Spirit you breathe into us,
    a wandering Spirit,
    for eyes that guide us,
    for feet that plod the paths,
    for occasional signposts when we have lost our way.

We thank you for your love
    which gives our journey meaning and direction.
You bless us with your divine restlessness.
You prod us from our complacency.
You urge us down roads
    we do not feel strong enough to travel.
You support us with companions
    who bolster us when we despair,
    who refresh and renew us
    when we think our last step is just that.

For all those pilgrims who have gone before us
    and pointed the way to you,
    for Noah, Abraham and Sarah, Miriam and Moses,
    for David, Ruth, Esther, Solomon and Isaiah,
we give you thanks.

But most of all we thank you
for your greatest pilgrim, Jesus Christ,
    who is the way, the truth, and the life;
    who lights our path; who opens our eyes;
    who does not abandon us in our need;
    whose journey led him to Jerusalem;
    who there strengthened us with a meal
    to follow in his footsteps.

On the night before he died,
Jesus took bread and blessed you,
    then gave it to his friends with these words:
Here is food for the journey.
Take this, all of you, and eat.
This is my body given up for you.
Jesus later took a cup of wine.
Again he blessed you
    and gave it to his friends with these words:
Here is drink for the journey.
Take this and share it.
This is the cup of my blood,
    the new and everlasting covenant.
It is shed for you and all people
    so sins may be forgiven.
Do this in memory of me.

And so we thank you
    for the words and example of your pilgrim, Jesus.
By whose life you teach us
    to believe in you and life's journey.
By whose death you show us
    the meaning of hope when we lose everything.

And by whose resurrection you proclaim your love,
    which makes all weary, wrinkled pilgrims new.

So let us proclaim the mystery of our faith:
    Dying, you destroyed our death;
    rising, you restored our life.
Lord Jesus, come in glory.

Send us your Spirit so that we, your pilgrims,
can have light for our eyes, strength for our limbs,
and companionship on an otherwise lonely journey.

Help us accept the gifts you have given us.
Teach us to use them as we struggle
    with the journey-out and the journey-in,
    with the mystery of your presence in us and our world.

May we seek you, meet you and know you as we travel along the way.

All this we ask through Jesus Christ,
who is our way to you.

Through whom,
with whom,
in whom,
in the unity of the Holy Spirit,
all glory and honor is yours,
Ever Present God,
forever and ever.
Amen.

Michael Moynahan, S.J., adapted

FEEDBACK FORM

While the following questions may be answered with a simple "yes" or "no," please elaborate where appropriate:

1.   Did this retreat help you to spend time present to God?

2.   What insights have come to you through this retreat?

3.   Do you feel that you connected with other participants in a meaningful way?

4.   Did the physical set-up provide a suitable retreat environment?

5.   Additional comments and suggestions:

SUPPLIES CHECKLIST

- *Listening Hearts*, a copy for each participant
- copies of *Listening Hearts RETREAT DESIGNS* for all participants or else copies of all pages of this retreat design
- *Listening Hearts SONGBOOKS*
- music cassettes wound to correct side, unless a competent musician is available (for music cassettes, call the Christian Vocation Project, 410-225-9054)
- cassette player (or instrument[s] and musician[s])
- Bibles
- oil lamp or wide candle
- matches
- connected computer paper
- coloring pens
- pens or pencils
- clay (Plastilina No. 2, found in artist supply stores; otherwise plasticine.)
- paper plates
- chopsticks
- construction paper
- scissors
- Elmer's glue
- magazines with pictures, catalogs, newspapers, and perhaps fabric for collages

Introductory Segment for Optional Second Retreat

Hymn
"Spirit of the Living God"

Greetings

Introductions

Introduce yourself, giving your name and saying a few sentences about yourself. Use one of these questions as a lead-in:

- To what extent has discernment been part of your life?

- Are there areas in which you currently seek discernment?

- Do any factors impede discernment for you? Is any aspect of discernment especially difficult for you?

- How consciously have you tried to trace the movement of the Spirit through the years of your life?

- Have you ever thought you were following God's will and then realized with hindsight that you were mistaken?

- Are you aware of any reactions in yourself that seem to warn you when you are out of sync with God?

PLEASE STATE WHEN YOU HAVE FINISHED.

Retreat on Community

OBJECTIVES

To develop a deeper sense of the meaning and value of Christian community.
To spend time present to God.

CONTENTS

ORIENTATION SESSION

Hymn
"Spirit, Be Our Spirit"

Greetings

Introductions

In no particular sequence, please introduce yourself by name and briefly respond to some of the following questions:

Has a group of Christians ever

- helped you to experience God's presence?

- made it easier for you to sense what God wanted of you?

- made it more difficult for you to know what God wanted of you?

- made it easier for you to live out a call?

- made it more difficult for you to live out a call?

What thoughts and feelings come to you as you reflect on your responses to these questions?

Chant
"We Are in God Made One"

Overview

Presentation of Meditation Options

Hymn
"Jacob's Ladder Sequel"

FORMAT FOR RETREAT SESSIONS ON COMMUNITY

CHANT

"We Are In God Made One"

GATHERING SILENCE
(between five and fifteen minutes)

Glance back over Chapters 6 through 9 of *Listening Hearts.* Review portions you have marked, letting them permeate your consciousness. During this silence, you may offer reflections aloud if so moved.

CHANT

"We Are in God Made One"

HOUR OF MEDITATION

Go off in silence to meditate, following the guidelines for your selected option.

RE-GATHER

Quietly come back together to briefly share reflections arising from the hour of meditation.

CLOSING PRAYERS

Offer your prayers, silently or aloud.

THOMAS MERTON PRAYER

This prayer, at the very end of *Listening Hearts,* can be read corporately or by a different person each session.

CLOSING HYMN

"Jacob's Ladder Sequel"

OVERVIEW OF MEDITATION OPTIONS

This retreat provides for one extended meditation exercise that continues for multiple sessions, with the book *Listening Hearts* as a foundation. A text from Scripture will be the keystone. Each participant needs to pre-select one of three meditation options for the weekend:

OPTION 1:   **Contemplative Sand Tray**

Develop, tend, and behold a simple arrangement of small rocks and moss in a tray of sand.

OPTION 2:   **Mobile Meditation Exercise**

Construct a mobile that draws together your reflections on Christian community.

OPTION 3:   **Assorted Meditation Exercises**

For each session choose a meditation exercise from a variety of possibilities that involve writing, walking, and art.

People develop into a community not merely by interacting, but also as they come together at the Center.

"... I, Yahweh, speak with directness
I express myself with clarity." Assemble, come, gather
together...consult with each other....
Isaiah 45:19, 20, 21 (JB)

Where two or three are gathered in my name, there am
I in the midst of them. Matt. 18:20 (RSV)

. . . the saints together make a unity in the work of
service, building up the body of Christ.
Eph. 4:13 (JB)

Let us consider how to stir up one another to love and
good works, not neglecting to meet together . . . but
encouraging one another. Heb. 10:24-25 (RSV)

Now the whole group of those who believed were of one
heart and soul. . . . Acts 4:32 (NRSV)

Moses' father-in-law said to him, "What you are doing
is not good. You will surely wear yourself out, both
you and these people with you. For the task is too
heavy for you; you cannot do it alone."
Exod. 18:17-18 (NRSV)

The whole body is fitted and joined together, every
joint adding its own strength. Eph. 4:16 (JB)

... they called the church together and related all that
God had done with them. . . .
Acts 14:27 (NRSV)

OPTION 1
INSTRUCTIONS FOR CONTEMPLATIVE SAND TRAY

1. Procure your tray for sand: a sturdy rectangular container about ten by eighteen inches, and about three or four inches deep. Seal any crevices through which sand could leak. (Two possible ways to do this are by plugging any openings with sand and glue or by applying duct tape.)

2. Select one or possibly two Scripture passages from the list provided. Read your selected text over and over at the beginning of each meditation hour. Repeat it to yourself often during the course of the retreat.

3. Although it is not necessary, you may line the inside edges of the tray with some natural substance to form a wall or fence to frame your arrangement.

4. Slowly and reverently pour sand about two inches deep into the tray. Smooth it out gently.

5. Try to develop a feeling for what God may be saying to you through *Listening Hearts* and your Scripture text. Begin to write down a list of descriptive words that capture a sense of your thoughts and feelings; add to it as the retreat progresses.

6. Consider what kinds of rocks you want to look for — qualities you would like them to have, possible ways to group them.

7. Contemplatively walk about looking for rocks and moss. Find rocks that suggest things you want to express. Use your senses to feel that you yourself are each rock you select. Develop a sense of unity with the rocks. Touch them. Sit and look at them. Do the same with the moss.

8. Plant the rocks you select in your sand garden. Place them with care. Look for the right surfaces to show. Choose the best angles at which to place them. Bury part of each rock beneath the surface of the sand to embed it solidly so that it seems to grow out of the soil.

9.   Mold mosses, perhaps at the base of a rock or as part of an arrangement of rocks.

10.   Alternate between arranging materials and simply looking at what you are arranging. Fetch more rocks and moss as needed.

11.   Rake the sand in designs to suggest water. Possibilities include: Stylized waves. Straight parallel lines. Concentric circles. Swirls. Ripples. Clashing angles.

12.   Prepare a setting for your sand garden tray. Perhaps nestle it into an inviting spot outdoors. Or construct a suitable setting indoors by collecting appropriate foliage to arrange outside the tray along two or three sides.

13.   Spend time gazing at your arrangement. Let God touch you through it. Tend it. Be still with it. Be with God.

GENERAL SUGGESTIONS FOR SAND TRAY AND ROCK GARDEN

1. Move about slowly, feeling a sense of reverence for the ground beneath you, the air around you, the sky above you, and the wonder of God's creation.

2. Move your hands and arms contemplatively, sensing the sacredness of all you touch.

3. Feel the sand with its history and associations.

4. Look at the stones and rocks. Feel them. Notice their shapes, colors, textures, cracks, crevices, and angles. Select rocks that look and feel interesting, that suggest feelings and qualities you want to express. Rocks can convey strength, energy, movement, or stillness. Asymmetrical rocks generally evoke more response.

5. Odd numbers of rocks in a cluster and odd numbers of clusters usually provide the best opportunity to create balance and harmony within and among groupings.

6. Simple, uncluttered arrangements often produce images that are more intense.

7. Contrasting elements, irregular shapes, varied angles and textures help make compositions expressive.

8. Consider proportions. As you assemble the various elements, observe your composition from different perspectives.

9. Dampen the sand in order to rake it and shape it.

10. Do not rush. Remember that the real objective is to be with God rather than to complete a project.

OPTION 2
INSTRUCTIONS FOR MOBILE MEDITATION EXERCISE

1. Select a Scripture text from the list of passages on Christian community.

2. Using a prayer ring as a centering device, either sit quietly or walk for a while — repeating your Scripture passage over and over.

3. Then begin to reflect on your own experience of community life in relation to the selected text, slowly collecting objects that express your thoughts and feelings. Do not rush. Let your reflections evolve; give them time to sink in.

4. Eventually settle into a suitable spot with the physical symbols you have gathered. Use these materials and the supplies provided (rods, wire, fishline) to assemble a mobile. Construct the mobile contemplatively: observe relationships; consider balance; take time to absorb insights.

OPTION 3
INSTRUCTIONS FOR ASSORTED MEDITATION EXERCISES

SELECT ONE SCRIPTURE PASSAGE ABOUT CHRISTIAN COMMUNITY AS YOUR TEXT FOR THE ENTIRE RETREAT. THEN SELECT ONE OF THE MEDITATION EXERCISES FROM THE FOLLOWING LIST AT THE BEGINNING OF EACH SESSION. YOU MAY CHOOSE TO CONTINUE WITH ONE EXERCISE FOR MORE THAN ONE SESSION.

#1
W A L K

Take a prayer ring to wear on your finger and place its cross in the palm of your hand. Repeat your Scripture text over and over, eventually zeroing in on a few words or even a single word. Then set out for a walk. Use the prayer ring to keep yourself centered. Keep repeating the word or words that you distilled from your text. Keep your Scripture passage close to your heart. Let God touch you through the word or words. Stop to rest any time you want. Use this hour as an opportunity for these holy words to take root in your being. Take a time piece along so that you can get back to the group in time.

#2
D R A W

Take a number of pieces of connected computer paper and some coloring pens or crayons. Take *Listening Hearts* with you. Find a quiet comfortable place to draw. Spend some time looking back over the "Community" section of the book. Then begin to express your feelings on the first sheet of paper, using the pens or crayons. Express your feelings through movement and color and shapes. Do not concern yourself with artistic merit.

When you finish with the first sheet, stop and look at it for a while. Wait. Then either move on to draw on the second sheet or return to *Listening Hearts* for a while and then go back to drawing. Continue in this manner, progressing from one sheet to the next. Allow enough time at the end to open up the pages and look at the series of drawings for a while and then to get back to the group by the end of the hour.

3

MAKE A COLLAGE

Quietly go about, looking for things for your collage — things from nature, manufactured items, words and pictures from magazines that convey reflections that arise from *Listening Hearts* and your Scripture text. Arrange them on paper, cardboard, or a wooden board to express your thoughts and feelings.

#4
WRITE A HYMN

Select a familiar tune, sacred or secular. You may want to use a hymnal so that you have the music to look at. Using portions of Chapters 6 through 9 of *Listening Hearts* as a springboard, write a hymn to the tune you choose.

#5
MOLD CLAY

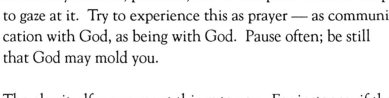

Take clay with a plate on which to work and a chopstick for etching it. Find a comfortable place to meditate with the clay.

As you reflect on Christian community, express your feelings in the clay: Press it, pound it, roll it. Shape it. Feel it. Stop to gaze at it. Try to experience this as prayer — as communication with God, as being with God. Pause often; be still that God may mold you.

The clay itself may suggest things to you. For instance, if the clay is hard to work with, but then becomes more supple from the warmth of your touch, that may say something to you.

#6
WRITE A SERIES OF QUESTIONS & RESPONSES

As you look back over Chapters 6 through 9 of *Listening Hearts*, make a list of questions that come to your mind: questions about discerning call in community, questions about your feelings, questions about your own experience. Then reflect on the questions one at a time, writing a stream-of-consciousness passage to go with each one.

#7
WRITE A POEM OR MEDITATION

Write a poem or meditation that ponders how your own life has evolved through Christian community.

CLOSING EUCHARIST

HYMN   *"God, You Dwell Here with Us"*

THOMAS MERTON PRAYER

Stand to read. Begin with "Let us pray."
Read the Thomas Merton Prayer on the last
page of *Listening Hearts*.

READINGS:
1. 1 Corinthians 12:4-27
2. Matthew 18:19-20

Readers stand to read. Announce the
reading and invite people to follow it in their
Bibles. Give people time to find the passage.
Conclude with "This is the word of the Lord."

REFLECTION PERIOD

An appointed person invites the group to
reflect on the Scripture passages in relation to
their meditations in the course of the retreat
and to offer their thoughts and feelings aloud
if so moved. Allows time for people to reflect
and to speak. Then concludes by standing and
offering a prayer that ties together the
Scripture and the reflection time, punctuated
with a loud "AMEN" at the end.

CHANT   *"Be Still and Know"*

PRAYERS

An appointed person invites the congregation
to offer their prayers, silently or aloud.
Permits time for free and open participation.
Then draws the prayers together in some
way, concluding with a hearty "AMEN."

PEACE

Presiding priest initiates by proclaiming:
"The peace of the Lord be always with you."

OFFERTORY:
Bread & Wine

One person presents bread as another
presents the water and wine.

Doxology

GREAT THANKSGIVING   "Incarnation"

LORD'S PRAYER

COMMUNION

THANKSGIVING FOR COMMUNION   Appointed person offers a short prayer of
                                    thanks for Communion.

HYMN   *"Holy Ground"*

DISMISSAL   As a charge to the congregation, the appointed
                                    person offers two or three sentences that
                                    capture the thrust of the weekend and
                                    challenge participants to take the message of
                                    the retreat into their daily lives. Concludes
                                    with "Go in peace, rejoicing in the power of
                                    the Spirit."

GREAT THANKSGIVING: INCARNATION

Magnanimous God, we gather together
    and give you thanks
    for all the wonders of your love.

We thank you for all the signs of your love in our lives,
    which are more numerous than the grains of sandy beaches.

But especially, we thank you
    for speaking your Word, Jesus Christ, to us.
You could have shown no greater love than by sharing
    what you treasured most, Jesus Christ, your only child,
    your Word of love, the hope to which we cling.

We thank you for speaking your word despite our deafness,
    for putting your word in our stubborn hearts.

Your word is life in many ways.
It comes through people in a forgiving word, a reassuring smile;
    it comes through those who walk mysteriously into our lives
    and awaken good in us we never knew existed,
    who elicit new insights, lighten dark places.

Your word is yes to who we are and all we do
    as we struggle to discover your presence
    in ourselves and our world.

We thank you for Jesus' life
    and all he taught us of your love.
And of all he said and did, we particularly thank you
    for the meal he shared and asked us to celebrate
    over and over until he comes again.
When he was at supper with friends, he took the bread,
    blessed you, and broke the bread, saying:
Take and eat.
This is my body broken for you.

Then he took the cup of wine,
    blessed you again,
    and passed it among them, saying:
Take and drink, all of you.
This is the cup of my blood
    poured out for all for the forgiveness of sins.
Do this in memory of me.

Send us your Spirit,
the Spirit of truth,
    to open our eyes and ears:
    to see you where we are afraid to look,
    to hear you in voices that offend our sensitive ears.

We seek you in the spectacular and extraordinary,
    and you come to us poor, hungry, thirsty, naked,
    diseased, in prison, alone, and as the least of our sisters and brothers.

Teach us to see you, hear you, touch you, know you,
    where you really are, and not where we would like you to be.

All this we ask through Christ, the Lord of Life.
Through whom,
with whom,
in whom,
in the unity of the Holy Spirit,
all glory and honor is yours,
Ever Present God,
forever and ever. Amen.

Michael Moynahan, S.J., adapted

FEEDBACK FORM

While the following questions may be answered with a simple "yes" or "no," please elaborate where appropriate:

1.   Have you developed any new insight into the meaning and value of Christian community?

2.   To what extent were you attuned to God's presence during this retreat? What aspects of the format were helpful in this regard? Which were not helpful?

3.   Additional comments and suggestions:

SUPPLIES CHECKLIST

- *Listening Hearts*, a copy for each person
- copies of *Listening Hearts RETREAT DESIGNS* for all participants or copies of all relevant pages
- *Listening Hearts SONGBOOKS* for each person
- music cassettes of accompaniment if needed (for music cassettes, call the Christian Vocation Project, 410-225-9054)
- cassette player, if needed
- Bibles
- rectangular containers about 8 by 10 inches and 3 or 4 inches deep to use as sand trays (corrugated box tops or baking tins are possibilities)
- fine sand
- a variety of wide-tooth teasing combs for raking
- small metal or wooden rods for mobiles (possibly from a plant nursery)
- thin wire
- clear plastic fishline
- clippers for wire
- scissors
- Elmer's glue
- construction paper
- colored yarns
- button thread
- wide-eyed needles
- picture magazines
- newspapers
- connected computer paper
- felt-tip coloring pens
- clay (Plastilina No. 2, found in artist supply stores; otherwise plasticine.)
- paper plates
- chopsticks
- wooden prayer rings (available at Catholic supply stores)

Group Rock Garden
a Self-conducted Retreat for 3, 4, or 5 People

OBJECTIVES

To develop a stronger sense of the meaning and value of spiritual community.
To consciously experience the formation of community in Christ.
To spend time centered in God.

Listening Hearts Group Rock Garden

CONTENTS

THE TASK

Together with others construct, contemplate, and care for a garden of rocks, moss, natural wood, water, and perhaps a few small plants in a box of sand.

Planning the "*Listening Hearts* Group Rock Garden"

1.   Recruit the participants.

2.   Decide on dates and meeting places.

3.   Make arrangements for the use of the agreed-upon meeting place.

4.   Make sure that each participant has a copy of *Listening Hearts* to read prior to the retreat.

5.   Distribute the retreat material ahead of time so that each person is familiar with the entire plan upon arrival. Each participant will need a copy of this book of *Listening Hearts RETREAT DESIGNS* or else copies of all of the relevant pages as enumerated on the Supplies Checklist.

6.   Procure the supplies listed on the Supplies Checklist. Deliver them to the meeting place.

7.   Either arrange for one of the participants to lead the singing or else get a cassette player and music cassettes of accompaniment for the two hymns. Music cassettes are available. Contact the Christian Vocation Project, 410-225-9054.

8.   Make arrangements for dinner. It can be supper in a home or a covered-dish supper at a church facility. Or the group can meet for dinner at a restaurant.

Introductory Questions To Consider During Dinner

Has a group of Christians ever

- helped you to experience God's presence?

- made it easier for you to sense what God wanted of you?

- made it more difficult for you to know what God wanted of you?

- made it easier for you to live out a call?

- made it more difficult for you to live out a call?

What thoughts and feelings come to you as you reflect on your responses to these questions?

INSTRUCTIONS FOR GROUP ROCK GARDEN

Prior to the retreat, read all of the instruction sheets. Also read the book <u>Listening Hearts</u>, particularly the section on "Community." Mark passages that especially catch your attention.

Friday Evening

1.   The retreat begins on Friday evening with dinner.

2.   At dinner, use the "Introductory Questions to Consider During Dinner" to stimulate dialogue.

3.   After dinner, take a short break and then gather at the agreed-upon meeting place.

4.   Chant *"We Are in God Made One"* several times over.

5.   Look over the list of Scripture passages. Together, select one or two to serve as the meditation text for your group.

6.   Take five minutes of silence to assimilate the passage(s).

7.   Consider whether the group wants to share the leadership or designate one person as convener.

8.   Develop consensus on group norms. Some possibilities:

   •   Try to listen to each other with your entire selves (senses, feelings, intuition, and rational faculties).

   •   Speak for yourself only, expressing your own thoughts and feelings, referring to your own experiences. Avoid being hypothetical or purely intellectual.

   •   Do not challenge what others say.

   •   Do not interrupt.

   •   Do not formulate what you want to say while someone else is speaking.

   •   Pause between speakers to absorb what has been said.

9.   Take some time to reflect on your Scripture text in relation to your life experience, articulating your thoughts and feelings as they surface.

10.   As a group, gradually let what you want to express through the garden begin to emerge. Record qualities you want to portray, feelings you want to express, paradoxes you want to convey, insights to which you want to give concrete form.

11.   Consider how the garden might be constructed to transmit these musings.

12.   About five minutes before 9 o'clock, begin to wind down, and then have someone read aloud the Thomas Merton Prayer at the very end of *Listening Hearts*.

13.   Conclude the evening session by singing the hymn *"Jacob's Ladder Sequel."*

Saturday

1.   Bring a bag lunch with you.

2.   Re-convene in the meeting place at 9 a.m.

3.   Chant *"We Are in God Made One"* several times over.

4.   Take five or ten minutes in silence to glance back over Chapters 6 through 9 of *Listening Hearts*. Review portions that you have marked, allowing them to penetrate your consciousness.

5.   Then take time to share aloud reflections that arise from these chapters.

6.   Silently re-read the "General Suggestions for Sand Tray and Rock Garden."

7.   Each person should then select a place to go to collect rocks and other natural materials. Locations with brooks or rivers are good areas in which to find interesting rocks and stones. Woods often have good mosses. Choose your destinations thoughtfully.

8.   Conclude this portion no later than 10 o'clock by chanting again *"We Are in God Made One."*

9.   Disperse to contemplatively gather natural materials for the garden: Rocks. Natural wood. Small plants. Moss. Water. (Clay is provided for building a lake, pond, pool, or channel of water.) Take your lunch with you. Collect more materials than you need so that you will be able to try different arrangements and make choices.

10.   Quietly return at 2:30. Chant *"We Are in God Made One."* Slowly begin to assemble a garden. Perhaps try to construct the garden without speaking verbally. At the very least, try to speak sparingly and communicate by observing visually. Move slowly. Arrange things reverently. Take time to be still and know that God is. Remember that empty space can be important for healthy community. Seek simplicity. Alternate between working on the garden and simply sitting. Remember that the purpose is not to complete a project, but to spend time close to God, yourself, and others.

11.   The clay can be used to mound the sand and/or hold water. The "walls" need to be thick to keep the water from seeping out.

12. Implant things securely to convey stability — what is beneath the surface can be as significant as what is visible above the surface.

13. You may want to construct a bridge or bridges. One way to do this is to find one or two flat, slightly arched rocks. Another possibility is to use clay and wood. Use rocks to build a solid base. Bridges can be important to forming community.

14. When you complete the garden, care for it as needed. Enjoy it. Let God speak to you through it. Be quiet with it. Share reflections.

15. At 4:30, begin to look back on the entire experience. Articulate insights and observations. Think about anything you may have learned about yourself and about Christian community. Offer prayers if moved to do so.

16. At 4:50 conclude by singing *"Jacob's Ladder Sequel."*

17. Fill out the feedback forms before departing.

The group may amend these guidelines in any way the Spirit seems to move them through Quaker consensus (see *Listening Hearts*, Chapter Seven).

FEEDBACK FORM

While the following questions may be answered with a simple "yes" or "no," please elaborate where appropriate:

1. Was this retreat an experience of spiritual community for you?

2. Have you developed any new insight into the meaning and value of Christian community?

3. To what extent were you attuned to God's presence during this retreat? What aspects of the format were helpful in this regard? Which were not helpful?

4. Additional comments and suggestions:

SUPPLIES CHECKLIST

- *Listening Hearts*, a copy for each participant
- a copy of *Listening Hearts RETREAT DESIGNS* for each person or
  copies of all relevant sheets:
  - Cover Page
  - Contents Page/The Task
  - Planning the *"Listening Hearts* Group Rock Garden"
  - Introductory Questions to Consider During Dinner
  - Instructions for Group Rock Garden
  - Selected Scripture Passages about Christian Community
    (from "Retreat on Community" section)
  - General Suggestions for Sand Tray and Rock Garden
    (from "Retreat on Community" section)
  - Feedback Form
- *Listening Hearts* SONGBOOKS
- music cassettes for accompaniment, if needed (available from the
  Christian Vocation Project, 410-225-9054)
- cassette player, if needed
- a sandbox at least 3 feet long, 18 inches wide, and 6 inches deep
- at least 100 pounds of all-purpose coarse sand (can be purchased at building supply store)
- clay — enough to build a pond or channel of water and perhaps a hill
- implements for raking sand: children's rakes, hand garden tools, styling
  combs with curved teeth, wooden cooking forks

LEADER GUIDELINES FOR SPECIFIC RETREATS

"*Listening Hearts* Retreat on Call, Ministry, and Discernment"

ORIENTATION SESSION (Friday evening)

GREETINGS
The leaders say a few words of welcome to the group to make them feel comfortable and to convey the intent, style, and tone of the retreat.

INTRODUCTIONS
This portion gives the leaders an opportunity to develop some feel for the group, helps the members of the group to get to know one another better, and eases people into the theme of the retreat. A leader may need to take the first turn at the introductions to give the members time to get their bearings.

OVERVIEW
In this section, the leader should carefully read aloud the retreat objectives listed on the cover page and then go over the format for the meditation sessions. Two terms need to be explained:

(1)   GATHERING TIME follows the opening hymn of each session. This is a silence of between five and fifteen minutes that gives the group time to become centered, to look back over the chapter, and to reflect on some of its contents. (It also gives anyone who has not read the book time to skim the chapter quickly, but encourage people to do their homework.) People who want to raise questions or elaborate on insights during this time may speak out.

(2)   SHARED REFLECTIONS is an opportunity for people to share the thoughts, feelings, and experiences that came to them during the meditation exercise they have just completed. It is not meant to be a time of discussion — which is to say, it is not a time to bat ideas back and forth or to challenge what others say. Normally, each person speaks only once; no one is required to speak. Preferably, participants do not comment on what others say during this time. Participants should try not to take more than their fair share of time.

The leader brings the time of Shared Reflections to a close by inviting people to offer their prayers, either silently or aloud, and then brings this period of informal prayers to a close by asking someone to read aloud the Thomas Merton Prayer found at the end of *Listening Hearts*.

Announcements provide an opportunity to clarify procedural details, to make sure the group knows the time the next session begins, and to emphasize any pieces of information that need to be reinforced.

SESSION: "THE INTRODUCTION"

It is intended that this portion follow the Orientation Session on Friday evening, to invite the group to slow down and open their hearts in preparation for the next day's meditation sessions. If the Orientation Session consumes the entire time available on Friday night, you may have to skip this section.

Suggest that people use the rest rooms during the exercise times rather than during the times they are together.

During the Orientation Session, you may want to take a little time to get a sense of how comfortable the group is with silence. Ask them how they feel about silence. Let them express their feelings and share their experiences, but try to keep it brief. Then try to build upon the positive: let them know that silence is an important ingredient in this program; encourage them to think of silence as a setting in which to listen to God with all the senses. You may want to say something about your own maturing in the use of silence. Be sure to listen to what they have to say so that you can gauge the amount of silence that you integrate into the retreat with a sensitivity to them.

If the Orientation Session takes a long time, a short silent break may be a good idea before beginning the session on the Introduction.

The exercises are planned as opportunities for solitude and silence. They will be more fruitful if people refrain from chatting. Make a special point of asking people to maintain silence during the exercise times. You may need to repeat this request at subsequent sessions.

THE INTRODUCTION (Friday evening)
Place an oil lamp without a chimney at the center of the circle to provide a focal point. The lamp can be placed on the floor or be put on a stool or low table. The wick should be adjusted, tested, and put in place before the group arrives. A wide candle may be used as a substitute. The leaders can light the lamp during the hymn "Be Still and Know."

Before beginning the exercise, inform the group of the sequence for the exercise: first you will read the quotation; then the group will have time to read the quotation silently to themselves several times over; then the lights will go out for a specified period of time, which the leader needs to decide upon and announce to the group. Determine the length of the silence to follow by considering both the group's comfort level with silence and the amount of time left before closing time. Five minutes should be an absolute minimum. Announce to the group how long the silence will be.

When the lights go back on, the group will chant "Stay Here and Keep Watch" several times through. Have them locate this hymn in the *Listening Hearts SONGBOOK* and mark it before starting. Ask if anyone has any questions.

Then ask them to turn to the exercise for the Introduction. Slowly read the quotation aloud. Then read the two sentences of instruction aloud.

Then repeat the two sentences of instruction and read the quotation once again. After one or two minutes, quietly turn the lights out (you will need to practice working the light switches before the group arrives).

To conclude the period of silence, turn the lights back on and begin the chant. After a few minutes of chanting, invite people to share their reflections.

THOMAS MERTON PRAYER
The Thomas Merton Prayer at the end of *Listening Hearts* is read every session. Ask a different participant to read it aloud each time. You may want to line up a reader prior to each session.

SUPPLIES
Before every session, lay out the material needed for the exercises. At the conclusion of each session, take an inventory to make sure you retrieve all your supplies.

FEEDBACK FORMS
At the conclusion of the retreat, permit sufficient time for people to fill out the feedback forms. It is important that people complete the forms before leaving — it is nearly impossible to get the forms back once people leave the premises.

FINAL HYMN
After the completed feedback forms have been collected, sing *"Jacob's Ladder Sequel"* as a finale.

DIVIDING A SESSION
In order to fit the retreat into given time slots, you may on occasion need to divide a session, doing part before a meal and the second part after a meal, or doing part one day and finishing it the next. This can be done by adding the concluding pieces after the Gathering Time:

> INFORMAL PRAYERS
> THOMAS MERTON PRAYER
> ANNOUNCEMENTS
> HYMN   *"We Know Not Where the Road Will Lead"*

Then, to provide an opening hymn for the next session, use *"Spirit Be Our Spirit."*

CONCLUDING A RETREAT

If a retreat is to end before getting to Chapter 5, you can provide a conclusion following the final hymn of whatever session you reached by adding a concluding portion that consists of

    CLOSING EUCHARIST (if desired)
    FEEDBACK FORMS
    HYMN   *"Jacob's Ladder Sequel"*

DIVIDING MATERIAL INTO TWO RETREATS

A retreat can be as short as one day or as long as two overnights. The best way to cover all of the material and keep a comfortable pace is to have one retreat that lasts two overnights, or else to divide the material into two successive retreats by concluding the first retreat after the session on "Discernment" and then covering Chapters 4 and 5 during the second retreat.

An introductory segment for a second retreat is provided in case the two-retreat option is selected. If a second retreat is offered, participation should be limited to people who have either attended the first retreat or else made a very firm commitment to thoroughly and prayerfully study the entire book *Listening Hearts*, including all of the appendices and endnotes.

BREAKING INTO SMALL GROUPS

If the size of the group is too large, you may divide into small groups for the times of Shared Reflections that follow the Meditation Exercises.

MEALS

Meals may be talking or silent, depending on the background and inclination of the group. The meditation session on Chapter 4 is a good one to schedule for immediately after lunch, since it calls for walking, which helps combat the drowsiness that often follows the midday meal.

TIME SCHEDULE

It is a good idea to prepare a time schedule, make copies, and distribute them so that participants can know what is coming.

ADHERE TO THE OBJECTIVES

Keep the objectives firmly in mind. Stay attentive to the Spirit. Be prayerful and fluid. If something is going unusually well, let it have some extra time and shave time off somewhere else. If something is not going well, move ahead more quickly and help avoid a time crunch elsewhere. Always try to be aware of the overall time-frame. Keep the objectives in your consciousness.

"Listening Hearts Retreat on Community"

This retreat is best held in a location where a variety of rocks are available. Streams and rivers are good places to look for rocks. Mild weather is preferable. Suggest foul-weather gear if needed.

DINNER OR REFRESHMENTS

Since Christian community is the theme of this retreat, make this meal or refreshment time as warm and hospitable as possible.

ORIENTATION SESSION (Friday evening)

GREETINGS

This is a time for the leader to welcome the group, say a few words about the theme, and set an informal, friendly tone.

INTRODUCTIONS

The introductions help people to get to know one another and give them a chance to begin to reflect on the theme of Christian community.

OVERVIEW

First make sure that everyone is aware of the objectives of the retreat listed on the cover page. Then go over the plan and schedule for the weekend, explaining that each person needs to select one meditation option to work with for the entire retreat. This makes one continuing meditation that builds from one session to the next. The format for each session is the same. Go over the format with the group.

PRESENTATION OF MEDITATION OPTIONS

Ask everyone to turn to the Overview of Meditation Options page and then either read the page aloud or paraphrase its contents. Everyone will need to select one option for the entire retreat before the first session in the morning. Page through the material with the group. Then let them glance through the instructions and ask questions while you say something about each option in an abbreviated form. Ask participants to read through the instructions more thoroughly after the evening session is over.

FORMAT FOR RETREAT SESSIONS ON COMMUNITY

Try to schedule at least four of these sessions. Each retreat session uses the same format and should last at least an hour and a half. An hour is allotted for the period of meditation at each session except for the final one. At the last session, the hour of meditation can be shortened to as little as ten minutes to permit ample time for people to report back on their meditations.